THE WINE QUOTATION BOOK

The Wine
Quotation Book

A Literary Celebration

Edited by

JENNIFER TAYLOR

ROBERT HALE · LONDON

Robert Hale Limited
Clerkenwell House
Clerkenwell Green
London EC1R 0HT

British Library Cataloguing in Publication Data

The wine quotation book : a literary celebration
1. Quotations in English. Special subjects. Wines
I. Taylor, Jennifer
808.88'2

ISBN 0-7090-3843-7

Photoset in Goudy by
Derek Doyle & Associates
Manufactured in Hong Kong by
Bookbuilders Ltd

Acknowledgements

The editor would like to thank the following agents and publishers for permission to quote from authors' work:

Jonathan Cape: Ernest Hemingway and Bernard Levin; Century Hutchinson: Duff Cooper and P.G. Wodehouse; Collins: John Arlott and Eric Newby; Fourth Estate: Auberon Waugh; Faber & Faber: Siegfried Sassoon; Grove Press Inc.: Frank Harris; Hamish Hamilton: Leonard Bernstein; A.M. Heath: Gerald Asher and George Orwell; Oxford University Press: Walter Shewring (Homer translations) and Ivan Morris (Sei Shonagon translation); New York *Vogue*: Evelyn Waugh; Peters, Fraser & Dunlop: John Mortimer, Cyril Ray and Evelyn Waugh; Murray Pollinger: Roald Dahl.

Preface

I should perhaps be claiming here that I have tippled since the cradle. I haven't, although I did have a French grandmother. Nor did doing the research for this book send me straight to the bottle, despite the many invitations to drink made down the centuries.

Wine, as the French gastronomer Brillat-Savarin observed, goes back to the childhood of the world; and rather a lot of wine has been drunk down the years. One could say that it has flowed like water – except that wine-drinkers show remarkable distaste for the stuff which, as everyone knows, 'ruins the palate'.

The chorus of praise for wine's qualities has been balanced by a chorus of lament for its less happy effects, for the dividing-line is a thin one, as so many people have found to their cost. Ovid's advice still stands good: do not drink till you see double, lisp or sleep. And Thomas Jefferson worked out some guidelines for himself which are pretty close to the limits set down by the medical profession today.

One of the delights in compiling this collection has been to find similar sentiments expressed by people living at different times. Pepys' inability to resist wine, and his ongoing remorse about it, is echoed by Parson Woodforde's wildly fluctuating consumption of port a century later.

The history of the wine trade is a fascinating one, as is the history of drinking-habits, and it is nice to find precedents for what seem like modern practices. The Beaujolais Nouveau craze is often dismissed by sniffy wine writers in the press as simply a marketing-inspired gimmick. But 11 November in France is not only St Martin's Day – the patron saint of reformed drunkards – but the feast of Bacchus, and the event was celebrated centuries back by a joyful tasting of the new wine, or as Rabelais called it, 'September pure'. It would come as no surprise to read in Pantagruel, *'Busvons, car Beaujolai Nousveau est arrisvé'.*

Any present-day scandals about the adulteration of wine can be bettered; brimstone does not seem any more desirable than antifreeze, and for a stomach-churning description it would be hard to beat Peter of Blois's words in the twelfth century.

Wine snobbery is a peculiarly English phenomenon, since the French on the whole prefer to get on with the business of eating and drinking. As in other European countries, wine is 'as natural and as necessary as bread', as many writers have demonstrated.

The British love affair with claret has been a long and literary one, and high-flown words have flowed in its praise – perhaps to pass away the time while it matures in the cellar – while the great claret/burgundy debate has inspired heady argument. Wine writers have certainly never been at a loss for words, enthusing about legendary Lafites and Richebourgs, about the joys of sherry, frothy champagne – which gave Mr Jorrocks such 'werry gentlemanly ideas' – and magisterial port. This selection certainly does not scrape the barrel.

Venite apotemus – come, let us drink – as Rabelais's monk enjoined. I'll settle for a modest Côte de Brouilly 1987.

JENNIFER TAYLOR

Wine, the most delightful of drinks, whether we owe it to Noah, who planted the vine, or to Bacchus, who pressed juice from the grape, goes back to the childhood of the world.

> BRILLAT-SAVARIN
> *La Physiologie du goût*

Wine is one of the most civilized things in the world and one of the natural things of the world that has been brought to the greatest perfection, and it offers a greater range for enjoyment and appreciation than, possibly, any other purely sensory thing.

> ERNEST HEMINGWAY
> *Death in the Afternoon*

Wine is a friend, wine is a joy; and, like sunshine, wine is the birthright of all.

> ANDRÉ SIMON
> *A Wine Primer*

God made only water, but man made wine.
VICTOR HUGO
Les Contemplations

Bacchus we thank who gave us wine
Which warms the blood within our veins;
That nectar is itself divine.
The man who drinks not, yet attains
By godly grace to human rank
Would be an angel if he drank.
PIERRE MOTIN
old French drinking song

If God forbade drinking, would He have made wine so good?
CARDINAL RICHELIEU

Wine … cheereth God and man.
JUDGES, 9:13

If Heaven did not love wine,
Then there would be no wine star in Heaven.
If Earth did not love wine
There would be no wine springs on earth –
Why then be ashamed before Heaven to love wine? …
Three cups, and one can perfectly understand the Great
Tao;
A gallon, and one is in accord with all nature.
LI T'AI PO
Chinese poet, in 740

And wine that maketh glad the heart of man, and oil to make his face to shine, and bread which strengtheneth man's heart.

PSALMS, 104:15

The smell of wine, oh how much more delicate, cheerful, gratifying, celestial and delicious it is than that of oil!

RABELAIS
Gargantua

And at that I came close to the Cyclops and spoke to him, while in my hands I held up an ivy-bowl brimmed with dark wine ... He took my present and drank it off and was mightily pleased with wine so fragrant. Then he asked for a second bowlful of it: 'Give me more in your courtesy, and tell me your name here and now ... Earth is bounteous, and for my people too it brings forth grapes that thrive on the rain of Zeus and that make good wine, but this is distilled from nectar and ambrosia.'

HOMER
The Odyssey

Wine is the drink of the gods, milk the drink of babies, tea the drink of women, and water the drink of beasts.

JOHN STUART BLACKIE
Scottish author, 19th century

Wine gives great pleasure; and every pleasure is of itself a good. It is a good, unless counterbalanced by evil.

SAMUEL JOHNSON
Boswell's *Life of Johnson*

12

Let us drink and be merry, dance, joke, and rejoice,
With claret and sherry, theorbo and voice!
THOMAS JORDAN
17th century

From wine what sudden friendship springs!
JOHN GAY
The Squire and His Cur

A man cannot make him laugh; – but that's no marvel; he
drinks no wine.
SHAKESPEARE
Henry IV Part 2

Fill ev'ry glass, for wine inspires us,
And fires us
With courage, love and joy.
Women and wine should life employ.
Is there aught else on earth desirous?
JOHN GAY
The Beggar's Opera

Here with a Loaf of Bread beneath the Bough,
A Flask of Wine, a Book of Verse – and Thou
Beside me singing in the Wilderness –
And Wilderness is Paradise enow.
The Rubáiyát of OMAR KHAYYÁM
translated by Edward FitzGerald

Wine comes in at the mouth
And love comes in at the eye;
That's all we shall know for truth
Before we grow old and die.
I lift the glass to my mouth,
I look at you, and I sigh.
  W.B. YEATS
  'A Drinking Song'

Who loves not wine, woman and song,
Remains a fool his whole life long.
  J.H. VOSS
  (long attributed to Martin Luther)

Let us have wine and women, mirth and laughter,
Sermons and soda-water the day after.
  BYRON
  Don Juan

Give me women, wine and snuff
Until I cry out 'hold, enough!'
You may do so sans objection
Till the day of resurrection;
For bless my beard they aye shall be
My beloved Trinity.
  KEATS
  'Women, Wine and Snuff'

I may not here omit those two main plagues and common dotages of human kind, wine and women, which have infatuated and besotted myriads of people; they go commonly together.

> ROBERT BURTON
> *Anatomy of Melancholy*

In the order named, these are the hardest to control: Wine, Women, and Song.

> FRANKLIN PIERCE ADAMS
> American humorist

Wine and wenches empty men's purses.

> ENGLISH PROVERB

Wine gives us liberty, love takes it away.
Wine makes us princes, love makes us beggars.

> WYCHERLEY
> *The Country Wife*

To see what wine and women can do, the one makes a man not to have a word to throw at a Dogge, the other makes a man to eat his owne words.

> DEKKER and WEBSTER
> *Westward Hoe*

God made man, frail as a bubble;
Man made love – love made trouble.
God made the vine –
Then is it a sin
That man made wine
To drown trouble in?

> ANON.

Now Arthur, flushed with a good deal of pride at the privilege of having the keys of the cellar ... had brought up a liberal supply of claret for the company's drinking, and ... he and the Curate began to pass the wine very freely.

One bottle speedily yielded up the ghost, another shed more than half its blood, before the two topers had been much more than half-an-hour together – Pen, with a hollow laugh and voice, had drunk off one bumper to the falsehood of women, and had said sardonically, that wine at any rate was a mistress who never deceived, and was sure to give a man a welcome ...

'You – you are taking too much wine, Arthur,' Mr Smirke said softly – 'you are exciting yourself.'

'No,' said Pen, 'women give headaches, but this don't.'

> THACKERAY
> *Pendennis*

Wine gives courage and makes men apt for passion.

> OVID
> *Ars Amatoria*

Wine lets no lover unrewarded go.

> ALEXANDER POPE
> *The Wife of Bath*

Miss Adams, alias Clayton, in Halkerston's Wynd – She is about 25 years of age, very agreeable, about the middle size, dark brown hair, fine eyes, remarkable good teeth and a tempting white bosom. She is likewise a firm votary to the wanton Goddess; and does not despise the God Bacchus, to whose rosy smiling cheeks she will often toss off a sparkling bumper.

> *Ranger's Impartial List of the Ladies of Pleasure in Edinburgh*, 1760s

Wine makes old wives wenches.
JOHN CLARKE
17th century

Wine is a precious aphrodisiac, and its fumes have blighted
many a mating.
NORMAN DOUGLAS
An Almanac

She believed he had been drinking too much of Mr
Weston's good wine, and felt sure that he would want to be
talking nonsense ... But Mr Elton had only drunk wine
enough to elevate his spirits, not at all to confuse his
intellects.
JANE AUSTEN
Emma

Wine and Love have ever been allies;
But carefully from all intemperance keep,
Nor drink till you see double, lisp or sleep.
OVID

I make love to good wine and to drinking.
ETIENNE PASQUIER
16th century

Where there is no wine, love perishes, and everything else
that is pleasant to man.
EURIPIDES
The Bacchae

While wine and friendship crown the board,
We'll sing the joys that both afford;
And he that won't with us comply,
Down among the dead men let him lie.
JOHN DYER
18th century

Wine is old men's milk.
THOMAS COGAN
The Haven of Health, 1584

Die I must, but let me die drinking in an inn!
Hold the wine-cup to my lips sparkling from the bin!
So, when angels flutter down to take me from my sin,
'Ah, God have mercy on this sot,' the cherubs will
begin.
WALTER DE MAP
12th century

... A ghost may come;
For it is a ghost's right,
His element is so fine
Being sharpened by his death,
To drink from the wine-breath
While our gross palates drink from the whole wine.
W.B. YEATS
'All Souls' Night'

Ah, with the Grape my fading Life provide,
And wash my Body whence the Life has died,
And in a Winding-sheet of Vine-leaf wrapt,
So bury me by some sweet Garden-side.

That ev'n my buried Ashes such a snare
of Vintage shall fling up into the Air,
As not a True believer passing by
But shall be overtaken unaware.
    The Rubáiyát of OMAR KHAYYÁM
    translated by Edward FitzGerald

A glass of good wine is a gracious creature, and reconciles
poor mortality to itself, and that is what few things can do.
    SIR WALTER SCOTT
    Journal

It is not for kings to drink wine; nor for princes strong
drink:
Lest they drink, and forget the law, and pervert the
judgment of any of the afflicted.
Give strong drink unto him that is ready to perish, and
wine unto those that be of heavy hearts.
Let him drink, and forget his poverty, and remember his
misery no more.
    PROVERBS, 31:4-7

Give me wine to wash me clean
Of the weather-stains of cares.
    R.W.EMERSON
    translated from the Persian

Give me a bowl of wine:
I have not that alacrity of spirit,
Nor cheer of mind, that I was wont to have.
    SHAKESPEARE
    Richard III

21

Wine can clear
The vapours of despair
And make us light as air.
   JOHN GAY
   The Beggar's Opera

Wine cheers the sad, revives the old, inspires
The young, makes weariness forget his toil,
And fears her danger; opens a new world
When this, the present, palls.
   BYRON
   Don Juan

I can truthfully say that since I reached the age of discretion I have consistently drunk more than most people would say was good for me. Nor do I regret it ... Often wine has shown me matters in their true perspective, and has, as though by the touch of a magic wand, reduced great disasters to small inconveniences.

Wine has lit up for me the pages of literature, and revealed in life romance lurking in the commonplace.

Wine has made me bold but not foolish; has induced me to say silly things but not to do them.

Under its influence words have often come too easily which had better not have been spoken, and letters have been written which had better not have been sent.

But if such small indiscretions standing in the debit column of wine's account were added up, they would amount to nothing in comparison with the vast accumulation on the credit side.
   DUFF COOPER
   Old Men Forget

When men drink wine they are rich, they are busy, they push lawsuits, they are happy, they help their friends.

ARISTOPHANES
The Knight

When they [wines] were good they pleased my sense, cheered my spirits, improved my moral and intellectual powers, besides enabling me to confer the same benefits on other people.

GEORGE SAINTSBURY
Notes on a Cellar-Book

Wine makes a man better pleased with himself. I do not say that it makes him more pleasing to others ... Wine gives a man nothing. It neither gives him knowledge nor wit; it only animates a man, and enables him to bring out what a dread of the company has repressed. It only puts in motion what has been locked up in frost. But this may be good, or it may be bad.

SAMUEL JOHNSON
Boswell's *Life of Johnson*

Wine is like rain: when it falls on the mire it but makes it the fouler,
But when it strikes the good soil wakes it to beauty and bloom.
JOHN HAY
Distichs

No draught of wine amid the old tombs under the violet sky but made me for the time a better man, larger of brain, more courageous, more gentle ... Could I but live for ever in thoughts and feelings such as those born to me in the shadow of the Italian vine!

> GEORGE GISSING
> *The Private Papers of Henry Ryecroft*

It is wine which brings out the worth of men and which sets apart from serfs those born free.

> PERSIAN SOURCE
> 10th century

In vino veritas – Truth comes out in wine.

> PLINY
> *Historia Naturalis*

Wine is the glass of the mind.

> ERASMUS

Wine brings to light the hidden secrets of the soul.

> HORACE
> *Epistles*

Oh! That second Bottle is the Sincerest, Wisest, and most Impartial, Downright Friend we have; tells us truth of ourselves, and forces us to speak Truths of Others; banishes Flattery from our Tongues, and distrust from our Hearts; sets us above the mean Policy of Court Prudence; which makes us lie to one another all Day, for fear of being betrayed by one another at Night. And ... I believe, the errantest Villain breathing, is honest as long as that Bottle lives.

> LORD ROCHESTER
> *Familiar Letters*

Wine it is the milk of Venus,
And the poet's horse accounted:
Ply it and you all are mounted.
BEN JONSON
verses over the door at the Devil Tavern

No poems can please nor live long which are written by water drinkers. Ever since Bacchus enrolled poets, as half-crazed, amongst his Satyrs and Fauns, the sweet Muses have usually smelt of wine in the morning…
HORACE
Epistles

When Horace wrote his noble verse,
His brilliant, glowing line,
He must have gone to bed the worse
For good Falernian wine.
THEODORE MAYNARD
A Tankard of Ale

Wine is bottled poetry.
ROBERT LOUIS STEVENSON

Poetry is devils' wine.
ST AUGUSTINE

I am health, I am heart, I am life!
For I give for the asking
The fire of my father, the Sun,
And the strength of my mother, the Earth.

Inspiration in essence,
I am wisdom and wit to the wise,
His visible muse to the poet,
The soul of desire to the lover,
The genius of laughter to all.
    W.E.HENLEY
    'Echoes'

Aristotle, that master of arts,
Had been but a dunce without wine,
And what we ascribe to his parts,
Is but due to the juice of the vine.
    ANON

Gude claret best keeps out the cauld,
And drives away the winter soon;
It maks a man baith gash and bauld
And heaves his saul beyond the moon.
    ALLAN RAMSAY
    18th century

There is not the hundredth part of the wine consumed in
this kingdom that there ought to be. Our foggy climate
wants help.
    JANE AUSTEN
    Northanger Abbey

O for a draught of vintage! that hath been
Cool'd a long age in the deep-delved earth,
Tasting of Flora and the country green,
Dance, and Provençal song, and sunburnt mirth!
    KEATS
    'Ode to a Nightingale'

The juice of the grape is the liquid quintessence of
concentrated sunbeams.
>
THOMAS LOVE PEACOCK

Drink wine in Winter for cold, and in Summer for heat.
>
H.G.BOHN
>
Handbook of Proverbs

Drink no longer water, but use a little wine for thy
stomach's sake and thine often infirmities.
>
1 TIMOTHY, 5:23

He that drinks not wine after salad, is in danger of being
sick.
>
COTGRAVE
>
17th century

Of all drinks wine is most profitable, of medicines most
pleasant, and of dainty viands most harmless ...
>
PLUTARCH
>
Morals

Wine can be considered with good reason as the most
healthful and the most hygienic of all beverages.
>
LOUIS PASTEUR

Drink a glass of wine after your soup, and you steal a rouble
from the doctor.
>
RUSSIAN PROVERB

Ripe, good old wine imparts a richer blood
To him who daily tastes its tonic flood.
SCHOOL OF SALERNO
Code of Health
11th century

Wine has the property of warming the innards when one drinks it, and of refreshing the exterior of the body when one washes in it.
PLINY
Historia Naturalis

Wine ... is a great increaser of the vital spirits: it very greatly comforteth a weak stomack, helpeth concoction, distribution and nutrition, mightily strengtheneth the natural heat, openeth obstruction, discusseth windiness ...
DR TOBIAS VENNER
17th century

Some drink, some drink here! Bring those chestnuts from the wood of Estrocz: with good new wine, you'll be composing some fine farts.
RABELAIS
Gargantua

Your stomach is your wine cellar; keep the stock small and cool.
CHARLES TOVEY
Wit, Wisdom and Morals, Distilled from Bacchus, 1878

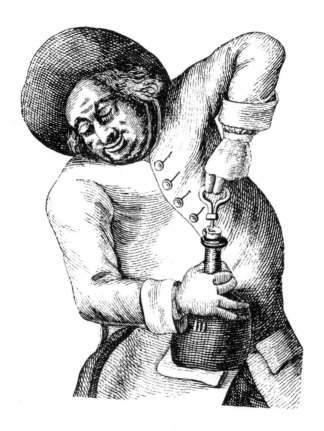

Like my friend the Doctor, I have lived temperately, eating little animal food... I double, however, the Doctor's glass and a half of wine, and even treble it with a friend; but halve its effects by drinking the weak wines only. The ardent wines I cannot drink... now retired... at the age of seventy-six.

> THOMAS JEFFERSON
> in a letter in March 1819

Place a substantial meal before a tired man, and he will eat with effort and be little better for it at first. Give him a glass of wine or brandy, and immediately he feels better: you see him come to life again before you.

> BRILLAT-SAVARIN
> *La Physiologie du goût*

Lazarus, you are more indebted to wine than to your father, for he gave you life but once, while wine has given it back to you a thousand times.

> SPANISH SOURCE
> 16th century

Have you noticed how bread tastes when you have been hungry for a long time? ... Jesus Christ, how good it was! As for the wine, I sucked it all down in one draught, and it seemed to go straight into my veins and flow round my body like new blood.

> GEORGE ORWELL
> *Down and Out in Paris and London*

Wine... is a food.
>   OLIVER WENDELL HOLMES
>   to the Massachusetts Medical Society in 1860

'My dear ... I have just recollected that I have some of the finest old Constantia wine in the house that was ever tasted ... so I have brought a glass of it for your sister. My poor husband! How fond he was of it! Whenever he had a touch of his old cholicky gout, he said it did him more good than anything else in the world. Do take it to your sister ...
>   JANE AUSTEN
>   *Sense and Sensibility*

Drink wine, and have the gout; drink none, and have the gout.
>   THOMAS COGAN
>   *The Haven of Health*, 1584

'Is anything the matter with Mr Snodgrass, sir?' inquired Emily, with great anxiety.

'Nothing the matter, ma'am,' replied the stranger. 'Cricket dinner – glorious party – capital songs – old port – claret – good – very good – wine, ma'am – wine.'

'It wasn't the wine,' murmured Mr Snodgrass, in a broken voice. 'It was the salmon.' (Somehow or other, it never *is* the wine, in these cases.)
>   CHARLES DICKENS
>   *The Pickwick Papers*

A heavy drinker was offered grapes at dessert. 'No thank you,' he said, pushing the dish away from him. 'I am not in the habit of taking my wine in the form of pills.'
>BRILLAT-SAVARIN
>*La Physiologie du goût*

When man eats the fruit of the vine he is as gentle as a lamb; when he drinks wine he believes himself a lion; if, by chance, he drinks too much he grimaces like a monkey; and when he is often drunk he is nothing more than a vile pig.
>THE TALMUD

Wine is a turncoat – first a friend, then an enemy.
>GEORGE HERBERT
>17th century

And Noah began to be an husbandman, and he planted a vineyard:
And he drank of the wine, and was drunken; and he was uncovered within his tent.
>GENESIS, 9:20-21

Bacchus, n. A convenient deity invented by the ancients as an excuse for getting drunk.
>AMBROSE BIERCE
>*Enlarged Devil's Dictionary*

Wine is a mocker, strong drink is raging: and whosoever is deceived thereby is not wise.
>PROVERBS, 20:1

Wine throws a Man out of himself, and infuses Qualities into the Mind which she is a Stranger to in her sober Moments. The Person you converse with, after the third Bottle, is not the same Man who first sat down at Table with you.

> JOSEPH ADDISON
> *Spectator*

Three cups of wine a prudent man may take:
The first of them for constitution sake;
The second to the girl he loves the best;
The third and last, to lull him to his rest –
Then home to bed. But if a fourth he pours,
That is the cup of folly, and not ours.
Loud noisy talking on the fifth attends;
The sixth breeds feuds and falling out of friends;
Seven beget blows, and faces stained with gore;
Eight, and the watch patrol breaks ope' the door;
Mad with the ninth, another cup goes round,
And the swilled sot drops senseless on the ground.

> ATHENAEUS
> *Deipnosophistae*

Some of the most dreadful mischiefs that afflict mankind proceed from wine; it is the cause of disease, quarrels, sedition, idleness, aversion to labour, and every species of domestic disorder.

> DE LA MOTHE FÉNELON
> 17th century

Wine heightens indifference into love, love into jealousy, and jealousy into madness; it often turns the good-natured man into an idiot, and the choleric man into an assassin. It gives bitterness to resentment, makes vanity insupportable, and displays every little spot of the soul in its utmost deformity.

JOSEPH ADDISON

Bacchus, that first from out the purple grape,
Crushed the sweet poison of misusèd wine.
JOHN MILTON
Comus

Who hath woe? Who hath sorrow? Who hath contentions? Who hath babbling? Who hath wounds without cause? Who hath redness of eyes? They that tarry long at the wine ...

PROVERBS, 13:29-30

The intemperate drinking of wine causes a chillness of the blood, a dissolution of the nerves, a dissipation of the generative seed, a numbness of the senses, a distortion of movement, which are all impediments to the act of generation. This is why you see Bacchus, king of drunkards, depicted beardless and in woman's dress, as an effeminate and ball-less eunuch.

RABELAIS
Pantagruel

'Tis pity wine should be so deleterious,
For tea and coffee leave us much more serious.
BYRON
Don Juan

When wine sinks, words soom [swim].
SCOTTISH PROVERB

Counsels in wine seldom prosper.
ENGLISH PROVERB

They [the Persians] are accustomed to deliberate on matters of the highest moment when warm with wine; but whatever they ... may determine is again proposed to them on the morrow, in their cooler moments. If at this time also it meet their approbation, it is executed; otherwise it is rejected. Whatever also they discuss when sober, is always a second time examined after they have been drinking.
HERODOTUS
Clio

In certain studies there is no harm in doing one's thinking and writing while slightly drunk, and then revising one's work in cold blood. The stimulus of wine is favorable to the play of invention, and to fluency of expression.
G.C.LICHTENBERG
Reflections
18th century

I think you told me, at Venice, that your spirits did not keep up without a little claret. I *can* drink, and bear a good deal of wine (as you may recollect in England): but it don't exhilarate – it makes me savage and suspicious. Laudanum has a similar effect; but I can take much of *it* without any effect at all. The thing that gives me the highest spirits (it seems absurd, but true) is a dose of *salts*.
BYRON
in a letter in 1821

It is wonderful what joy there is in excess. I stood it better today than yesterday. I came home not drunk though I had about two bottles of claret.

> JAMES BOSWELL
> *Diaries*, September 1779

Dined with the Colonel at his lodgings and as he was to be busy, just drank half a bottle of port ... I went to Fortune's, found nobody in the house but Captain James Gordon of Ellon. He and I drank five bottles of claret and were most profound politicians.

> JAMES BOSWELL
> *Diaries*, November 1774

At the first cup man drinks wine, at the second wine drinks wine, at the third wine drinks man.

> JAPANESE PROVERB

Let us drink to have wit, not to destroy it.

> PANARD
> French poet, 18th century

Wine hath drowned more men than the sea.

> THOMAS FULLER
> 17th century

So Noah, when he anchor'd safe on
The mountain's top, his lofty haven,
And all the passengers he bore
Were on the new world set ashore,
He made it next his chief design
To plant and propagate a vine,
Which since has overwhelm'd and drown'd
Far greater numbers, on dry ground,
Of wretched mankind, one by one,
Than all the flood before had done.
>   SAMUEL BUTLER
>   *Satire Upon Drunkenness*

Dyer laid Williams 2s. 6d, that he drank 3 Pints of Wine in 3 Hours, and that he wrote 5 verses out of the Bible right, but he lost ... He drank all the Wine, but could not write right for his Life. He was immensely drunk about 5 Minutes afterwards.
>   JAMES WOODFORDE
>   *The Diary of a Country Parson*, 4 November 1761

Whoever gulps down wine as a horse gulps down water is called a Scythian.
>   ATHENAEUS
>   *Deipnosophistae*

Life and wine for the likeness of nature are most agreeable. And this is the cause as I think why men by nature so greedily covet wine; except some odde Abstemius, one among a thousand perchance, degenerate and is of a doggish nature; for dogges of nature do abhor wine.
>   THOMAS COGAN
>   *The Haven of Health*, 1584

I hate the sight of men in their cups who shout, poke their fingers in their mouths, stroke their beards, and pass on the wine to their neighbours with great cries of 'Have some more! Drink up!' They tremble, shake their heads, twist their faces, and gesticulate like children ... I have seen really well-bred people behave like this and I find it most distasteful.

> THE PILLOW BOOK OF SEI SHONAGON
> 10th century
> translated by Ivan Morris

There is a devil in every berry of the grape.
> THE KORAN

Wine is the juice of the grape gone bad.
> LORD SOPER
> British clergyman

Where Satan cannot go in person, there he sends wine.
> JEWISH PROVERB

Take especial care that thou delight not in wine; for there never was any man that came to honour or preferment that loved it; for it transformeth a man into a beast, decayeth health, poisoneth the breath, destroyeth natural heat, deformeth the face, rotteth the teeth, and maketh a man contemptible.

> SIR WALTER RALEIGH
> *Instructions to His Son*

Wine is the first weapon that devils use in attacking the young.
> ST JEROME

Boys should abstain from all use of wine until their eighteenth year, for it is wrong to add fire to fire. But after forty years of age one can toast Dionysus with enthusiasm, for he gave wine to man to soften the bitterness of old age.

> PLATO
> *Laws*

There is not a corner nor burrow in all my body where this wine doth not ferret out my thirst.

> RABELAIS
> *Gargantua*

The wine in the bottle does not quench thirst.

> GEORGE HERBERT
> 17th century

Wine is the best liquor to wash glasses in.

> JONATHAN SWIFT

It is well to remember that there are five reasons for drinking: the arrival of a friend; one's present or future thirst; the excellence of the wine; or any other reason.

> LATIN SAYING

He said that few people had intellectual resources sufficient to forgo the pleasures of wine. They could not otherwise contrive how to fill the interval between dinner and supper.

> JAMES BOSWELL
> *Life of Johnson*

14 *May* 1661 Finding my head grow weak now-a-days, if I come to drink wine, and therefore hope that I shall leave it off of myself which I pray God I could do ...

26 July 1661 Having the beginning of this week made a vowe to myself to drink no wine this week (finding it to unfit me to look after business), and this day breaking of it against my will, I am much troubled for it – but I hope God will forgive me ...

29 September 1661, Lords Day At dinner and supper, I drank, I know not how, of my owne accord, so much wine, that I was even almost foxed and my head aked all night. So home, and to bed without prayers, which I never did yet since I came to the house of a Sunday night: I being now so out of order that I durst not read prayers, for fear of being perceived by my servants in what case I was. So to bed ...

26 January 1662 Thanks be to God, since my leaving drinking of wine, I do find myself much better, and do mind my business better, and so spend less money, and less time lost in idle company ...

    SAMUEL PEPYS
    Diary

I've heard him renounce wine a hundred times a day, but then it has been between as many glasses.

    DOUGLAS JERROLD
    19th century

Wine, n. Fermented grape-juice known to the Women's Christian Union as 'liquor', sometimes as 'rum'. Wine, madam, is God's next best gift to man.

    AMBROSE BIERCE
    Enlarged Devil's Dictionary

He found the key. He opened the cellar door. And there before him were bottles and bottles nestling in their bins, each one more than capable of restoring his mental outlook to its customary form. And he was in the very act of reaching out for the one nearest to hand when Linda's face seemed to rise before his eyes and he remembered his promise to her. 'Lay off the lotion', she had said to him, or words of that general import, and he had replied that he would. Even if the Archbishop of Canterbury were to come and beg him to join him in a few for the tonsils, he had said, no business would result.

P.G.WODEHOUSE
Frozen Assets

The dipsomaniac and the abstainer both make the same mistake: they both regard wine as a drug and not as a drink.

G.K.CHESTERTON

Wine was given us of God, not that we might be drunken, but that we might be sober; that we might be glad, not that we get ourselves pain.

ST JOHN CHRYSOSTOM
Homilies

Going back over the history of our own congregation, I've been struck by the huge amount of wine that was consumed at communion.... People didn't take a little sip of wine in the olden days, they took a big mouthful, and refreshed themselves, as it were.

REVD JAMES MARSHALL
in a radio interview

A glasse or two of wine extraordinarie would make a man praise God with much alacritie.

> NICHOLAS L'ESTRANGE
> 17th century

Good wine makes good blood,
Good blood causeth good humours,
Good humours cause good thoughts,
Good thoughts bring forth good works,
Good works carry a man to heaven.
Ergo,
Good wine carrieth a man to heaven.

> JOHN MINSHEU
> 16th century

Drink wine, and you will sleep well. Sleep, and you will not sin. Avoid sin, and you will be saved. *Ergo*, drink wine and be saved.

> MEDIEVAL GERMAN SAYING

The curé Ponosse vaguely imagined that in paradise time would be spent endlessly drinking the wine of Clochemerle.

> GABRIEL CHEVALLIER
> *Clochemerle*

The Grape that can with Logic absolute
The Two-and-Seventy jarring Sects confute ...

> *The Rubáiyát* of OMAR KHAYYÁM
> translated by Edward FitzGerald

One barrel of wine can work more miracles than a church full of saints.

> ITALIAN PROVERB

To drink wine is to be a good Catholic ... To drink only water, and to have a hatred for wine, is pure heresy close to atheism.

> BEROALDE DE VERVILLE
> 16th century

To happy convents, bosomed deep in vines,
Where slumber abbots, purple as their wines.
> ALEXANDER POPE
> *The Dunciad*

You yourself, my lord Prior, like to drink of the best. So does any honest man; never does a man of worth dislike good wine: it is a monastical apothegm.

> RABELAIS
> *Gargantua*

If wine disappeared from human production, I believe there would be, in the health and intellect of the planet, a void, a deficiency far more terrible than all the excesses and deviations for which wine is made responsible. Is it not reasonable to suggest that people who never drink wine, whether naïve or doctrinaire, are fools or hypocrites ...? A man who drinks only water has a secret to hide from his fellow-men.

> BAUDELAIRE
> *Du Vin et du hachish*

Wine is one of the noblest cordials in nature.
> JOHN WESLEY

No nation is drunken where wine is cheap; and none sober where the dearness of wine substitutes ardent spirits as the common beverage.

> THOMAS JEFFERSON
> *Writings*

I rejoice, as a moralist, at the prospect of a reduction of the duties on wine. It is an error to view a tax on that liquor as merely a tax on the rich. Prohibition of its use to the middling class is condemnation of them to poison whiskey.

> THOMAS JEFFERSON
> *Letters*, 1818

It is probably no exaggeration to state that we generally pay twice as much for our French wines as the Germans, Belgians, or Dutch, simply because they have a constant and large demand for the cheap wines of that country, and purchase the produce of whole vineyards in the state of grape, or just fermented, and charter vessels to carry it to their own cellars, while an English wine-merchant dares only venture to import a few hogsheads, and these generally at prices that foreigners never hear of.

> THOMAS GEORGE SHAW
> London wine merchant, a letter to *The Times* in 1851

Burgundy, Champagne, Bordeaux,
Would in many a goblet flow;
But the Custom House says, 'No,
You shan't drink light French wine,
You shan't drink light French wine.'

> Verses from *Punch* suggested by Mr Shaw's letters in 1851

If wine were made accessible to all classes in this country, temperance societies would soon be superfluous. For when the frugal meal of our humble labourer and artizan is cheered (as elsewhere) by a wholesome and invigorating beverage, drunkenness will gradually disappear.

Wine in Relation to Temperance, 1854

Grudge myself good wine? As soon grudge my horse corn.

THACKERAY

The government of the world I live in was not framed, like that of Britain, in after-dinner conversations over the wine.

HENRY DAVID THOREAU

There is a picture in mind of being on a very high-falutin' wine tour in Italy and looking out of the place from where the experts were tasting, across some farmland opposite; and there, an Italian labourer at his midday meal time picking the shelter of about the only tree within half a mile. Under the boughs he sat down with a great sausage sandwich and a bottle of wine. What a fool to wonder what the label was. Of course, there was no label. That was his wine, he made it – or his brother, or his uncle, father or grandfather: they drank wine automatically.

JOHN ARLOTT
Arlott on Wine

'The purpose of drinking wine is not intoxication, Rumpole .... The point of drinking wine is to get in touch with one of the major influences of western civilization, to taste sunlight trapped in a bottle, and to remember some stony slope in Tuscany or a village by the Gironde.'

I thought with a momentary distaste of the bit of barren soil, no doubt placed between the cowshed and the pissoir, where the Château Pommeroy grape struggles for existence.

JOHN MORTIMER
Rumpole and the Blind Tasting.

On my expressing great surprise that dung should be used at all in a vineyard of such reputation [Hermitage] ... the proprietor said that ... provided horse or sheep dung only were used, there was no danger of its giving the wine a bad flavour, though the contrary was the case if the dung of cows, and still more that of pigs, were made use of.

JAMES BUSBY
father of Australian wine, in *Journal of a Tour through some of the Vineyards of Spain and France,* 1834

Wine lives and dies; it has not only its hot youth, strong maturity and weary dotage, but also its seasonal changes, its mysterious, almost mystical, link with its parent vine, so that when the sap is running in the wood on the middle slopes of the Côte d'Or, in a thousand cellars, a thousand miles away the wine in its bottle quickens and responds.

EVELYN WAUGH
New York *Vogue,* 1937

Wine ... the blood of grapes.
GENESIS, 49:11

Pratt … had a curious, rather droll habit of referring to it [wine] as though it were a living being. 'A prudent wine,' he would say, 'rather diffident and evasive, but quite prudent.' Or, 'a good-humoured wine, benevolent and cheerful – slightly obscene, perhaps, but nonetheless good-humoured.'

> ROALD DAHL
> *Taste*

A bunch of grapes is beautiful, static and innocent. It is merely fruit. But when it is crushed it becomes an animal, for the crushed grapes become wine and wine has an animal life.

Wine suffers a heaving birth. It has a rough, groping childhood. It develops into adolescence. Then, if it does not sicken, it matures; and in this it is almost human since it does not mature according to a fixed rule but according to the law of its particular and individual personality.

> WILLIAM YOUNGER
> *Gods, Men and Wine*

There are no good wines, only good bottles.

> FRENCH SAYING

The alcohol in wine is as the canvas upon which an artist paints a picture …. It is not the small percentage of alcohol that appeals to you, but the brilliant ruby of the wine's colour, the attractive perfume of its bouquet and the delicious savour of its farewell, the lingering taste which it leaves behind as it descends smoothly down your grateful throat.

> ANDRÉ SIMON
> *A Wine Primer*

Nothing equals the joy of the drinker, except the joy of the wine in being drunk.

ANON.

Look not thou upon the wine when it is red, when it giveth his colour in the cup, when it moveth itself aright.

At the last it biteth like a serpent, and stingeth like an adder.

PROVERBS, 23:31-32

Is not old wine wholesomest, old pippins toothsomest, old wood burn brightest ...?

DEKKER and WEBSTER
Westward Hoe

No man also having drunk old wine straightway desireth new: for he saith, The old is better.

LUKE, 5:39

Wine kept for two or three years develops great poison.

CHINESE SOURCE
14th century

Good wine ruins the purse; bad wine ruins the stomach.

SPANISH PROVERB

There is no vine out of France to forreine country, save that which they brimstone a little, otherwise it would not keep on the sea, but it would spoil. It's true the wine works much of it out againe, yet this makes the wine much more unwholesome and heady than that we drink in the country wheir it growes at hand.

SIR JOHN LAUDER
Journals, 1665-76

A very inferior French wine, sold to the adulterators at a few sous the bottle, is now frequently mingled with rough cyder, and coloured to resemble claret, with cochineal, turnsole, and similar matters. This is pronounced fine quality, and sold as such in this country. Certain drugs are added as they appear to be wanted; and the medley, to which a large profit is attached, from the imposition, is frequently drunk without hesitation, and without any discovery of the cheat.

> quoted by THOMAS GEORGE SHAW
> *Wine, the Vine and the Cellar*, 1863

Bad wine does me no harm. Because it never gets past my nose.

> GEORGE SANDEMAN

'I rather like bad wine,' said Mr Mountchesney; 'one gets so bored with good wine.'

> BENJAMIN DISRAELI
> *Sybil*

The wine is turned sour or mouldy; thick, greasy, stale, flat and smacking of pitch. I have sometimes seen even great lords served with wine so muddy that a man must needs close his eyes and clench his teeth, wry-mouthed and shuddering.

> PETER OF BLOIS
> Archdeacon of London in the 12th century

Dinner at the Huntercombes' possessed only two dramatic features – the wine was a farce and the food a tragedy.

> ANTHONY POWELL
> *The Acceptance World*

The best use of bad wine is to drive away poor relations.
    FRENCH PROVERB

At one, dinner begins in the after-cabin – boiled salmon, boiled beef, boiled mutton, boiled cabbage, boiled potatoes, and parboiled wine ...
    THACKERAY
    Little Travels and Roadside Sketches

I beg you come tonight and dine
A welcome waits you and sound wine
The Roederer chilly to a charm
As Juno's breasts the claret warm ...
    J.B. ALDRICH

That little sentence 'have the chill taken off' has done more harm to good wine than it is possible to imagine.
    MARCEL BOULESTIN
    Simple French Cooking for English Homes

The English have a miraculous power of turning wine into water.
    OSCAR WILDE

Steer clear, I tell you, of both white and red
And in particular the white wine from Lepe
That's on sale in Fish Street and Cheapside.

This Spanish plonk somehow finds its crafty way
Into wines from nearby regions. And the kick
From just three cups of the resulting brew
Transports a chap who thinks he's safe at home
To sunny Spain! – in fact the town of Lepe.
  CHAUCER
  Pardoner's Tale

These traitorous thieves, accursed and unfair,
The vintners that put water in our wine.
  FRANÇOIS VILLON
  'A Merry Ballad of Vintners'

Wine has two defects: if you add water to it, you ruin it; if
you do not add water, it ruins you.
  SPANISH PROVERB

And Noah he often said to his wife when he sat down to
dine,
'I don't care where the water goes if it doesn't get into
the wine.'
  G.K.CHESTERTON
  'Wine and Water'

It was a very Corsican wine and you could dilute it by half
with water and still receive its message.
  ERNEST HEMINGWAY
  A Moveable Feast

With me I had a goatskin full of dark fragrant wine, given me by Maron, Euanthes' son ... unmixed and fragrant, a drink for the gods ... He would pour just one cupful of it into twenty measures of spring-water; from the mixing-bowl there would be wafted a fragrance beyond all words, and no one could find it in his heart to refrain.

> HOMER
> *The Odyssey*

The drinking of wine seems to have a moral edge over many pleasures and hobbies in that it promotes love of one's neighbour. As a general thing it is not a lone occupation. A bottle of wine begs to be shared; I have never met a miserly wine lover.

> CLIFTON FADIMAN
> *Any Number Can Play*

I like best the wine drunk at the cost of others.

> DIOGENES THE CYNIC

When you ask one friend to dine,
Give him your best wine!
When you ask two,
The second best will do!

> H.W.LONGFELLOW

You appear to have emptied your wine-cellar into your bookseller.

> THEODORE HOOK
> to a friend who made his publisher drunk at dinner

No good and worthy man will insist upon another man's drinking wine. As to the wine twenty years in the cellar, – of ten men, three say this, merely because they must say something; – three are telling a lie, when they say they have had the wine twenty years; – three would rather save the wine; – one, perhaps, cares.

SAMUEL JOHNSON
Boswell's *Life of Johnson*

A Wine Snob is a man ... who uses a knowledge of wine, often imperfect, to impress others with a sense of his superiority.

RAYMOND POSTGATE
The Plain Man's Guide to Wine

The wine snob is a product of enthusiasm. His interest in labels, châteaux and years ... is apt, however, to rob him of pleasure ... He frequently deprives himself – as no Frenchman, however wealthy in bottles and knowledge of wine, does – of the simple pleasure of humbly nameless but eminently drinkable French table wines.

JOHN ARLOTT
Arlott on Wine

Wine snobbery, of course, is part showmanship, part sophistication, part knowledge and part bluff.

LEONARD BERNSTEIN
The Official Guide to Wine Snobbery

For my part, I could not help thinking this lawyer was not such an invalid as he pretended to be. I observed he ate very heartily three times a day; and though his bottle was marked stomachic tincture, he had recourse to it so often, and seemed to swallow it with such peculiar relish, that I suspected it was not compounded in the apothecary's shop .... One day ... I dexterously exchanged the labels, and situation of his bottle and mine, and having tasted his tincture, found it was excellent claret.

> TOBIAS SMOLLETT
> *Humphrey Clinker*

The aristocrat of the table, the nature's gentleman of the cellar, the true *amateur*, the deeply knowledgeable, is rarely, if ever, a snob.

> MICHAEL BROADBENT
> *Wine Tasting*

An old wine-bibber having been smashed in a railway collision, some wine was poured on his lips, to revive him. 'Pauillac, 1873,' he murmured and died.

> AMBROSE BIERCE
> *Enlarged Devil's Dictionary*

At the first sip a good drinker should recognize the vintage, at the second the quality, and at the third the year.

> ALEXANDRE DUMAS
> *La Dame de Monsoreau*

Get a wineglass that exposes the wine to plenty of air. The more air you can expose wine to, the better you can taste it. And be sure you can get your nose in the glass. That's important because in wine-tasting, the nose does seventy-five per cent of the work. A glass with a three-inch brim is best for most wines. But if you have a larger than average nose, you'll need a larger than average glass.

INGLENOOK WINERY

As long as the wine is in the mouth, one receives a pleasant but indistinct impression; it is only when one has finished swallowing it that one can really taste, appreciate and identify its particular bouquet; and a short while must elapse before the gourmand can say: 'It's good, or passable, or bad. Bless my soul! It's Chambertin! Good grief! It's Suresnes!' ...

True connoisseurs *sip* their wine; for as they pause after each mouthful, they obtain the sum total of pleasure they would have experienced had they emptied the glass at a single draught.

BRILLAT-SAVARIN
La Physiologie du goût

I had just taken a swig of some smooth and velvety liquid that lingered in my mouth wih a distant memory of wild strawberries ...

'Over there, in case you're looking for it. Expectoration corner!' Bertie waved me to a wooden wine-box, half-filled with sawdust, into which the gents in dark suitings were directing mouthfuls of purplish liquid. I moved away from him, reluctant to admit that such wine as I had been able to win had long since disappeared down the little red lane.

JOHN MORTIMER
Rumpole and the Blind Tasting

The earlier stages of the dinner had worn off. The wine lists had been consulted, by some with the blank embarrassment of a schoolboy suddenly called on to locate a Minor Prophet in the tangled hinterland of the Old Testament, by others with the severe scrutiny which suggests that they have visited most of the higher-priced wines in their own homes and probed their family weaknesses.

> SAKI
> *The Chronicles of Clovis*

A sight of the label is worth fifty years' experience.

> MICHAEL BROADBENT
> *Wine Tasting*

One can learn about wine and pursue the education of one's palate with great enjoyment all of a lifetime ... even though the kidneys may weaken, the big toe become painful, the finger joints stiffen, until finally, just when you love it the most you are forbidden wine enirely ... I would rather have a palate that will give me the pleasure of enjoying completely a Château Margaux or a Haut Brion, even though excesses indulged in in the acquiring of it have brought a liver that will not allow me to drink Richebourg, Corton, or Chambertin, than to have the corrugated iron internals of my boyhood when all red wines were bitter except port and drinking was the process of getting down enough of anything to make you feel reckless.

> ERNEST HEMINGWAY
> *Death in the Afternoon*

When I am asked, as I sometimes am, what is the bottle of wine I have most enjoyed, I have to answer that it was probably some anonymous Italian *fiasco* that I drank one starlit Tyrrhenian night under a vine-covered arbour, while a Neapolitan fiddler played 'Come Back to Sorrento' over the veal cutlet of the young woman I had designs on...

For not only is taste in wine as subjective as taste in women, but its enjoyment depends more on circumstances than does that of almost any other pleasure.

CYRIL RAY
Ray on Wine

A bunch of us black-belt wine snobs were sitting around at dinner discussing some of the urgent social matters of the hour, like whether or not the '61 Latour was ready to drink ... The waiter arrived, and Reginald, our guiding spirit, ordered a Châteauneuf-du-Pape with mignonettes of lamb bordelaise. We turned to him aghast.

'Surely, Reginald, a red Bordeaux would be more compatible,' someone said.

'Possibly a Clos de Vougeot, or any good red Burgundy would be more subtle.'

'Perhaps even a Rhine,' I said, straining to appear both daring and sophisticated. '*Why* are you ordering a Châteauneuf-du-Pape?'

'Because I like the way it *sounds*,' said Reginald.

Indeed, it has been said of Châteauneuf-du-Pape that more bottles have been ordered because of the name than because of the wine... Wine snobs fear to admit it, but privately concede that they prefer the sound of a snappy Pouilly-Fuissé to a cumbersome and plodding Muscadet ...

Pouilly-Fuissé ... a charming, flutelike sound, like the

flight of a hummingbird or a quickly stolen kiss ... Amarone ... a wine of incredible depth, bouquet and breed. Forget about that, however, and listen to the name – preferably pronounced by Luciano Pavarotti – Am-mahr-roh-nay; a siren song, a seduction.

> LEONARD BERNSTEIN
> *The Official Guide to Wine Snobbery*

Sweetbreads financière and a bottle of mature Montrachet are not to be eschewed. But when I sit down to a plain daube of lamb and a bottle of Côtes du Rhône, I know that God's in his heaven, and all's right with the world.

> GERALD ASHER
> *On Wine*

For a gourmet wine is not a drink but a condiment, provided that your host has chosen it correctly.

> EDOUARD DE POMIANE
> *Cooking with Pomiane*

White meat, white wine; red meat, red wine.

> FRENCH PROVERB

After melon, wine is a felon.

> ITALIAN PROVERB

With cheese every kind of wine is acceptable, so it may truly be called *le biscuit des ivrognes*.

> GRIMOD DE LA REYNIÈRE
> *Almanach des gourmands*

There are no rules about the drinking and serving of wine such as might have been brought down by Moses ...

There is no reason why we should not ... if we disagree with our great-grandfathers, drink our white wine tepid, our red wine with lumps of ice in it, and wash down *sole Normande* with vintage port.

CYRIL RAY
Ray on Wine

In the year xxx Good wine of the large irrigated terrain of the Temple of Rameses II in Per-Amon. The chief of the wine-dressers, Tutmes.

EGYPTIAN WINE LABEL

Five qualities there are wine's praise advancing: Strong, beautiful, fragrant, cool and dancing.

JOHN HARINGTON
17th century

No. 699 Nuits, 1858, thin
" 870 Ditto, 1859, don't like
" 692 Vosne, 1858, full, fine, great bouquet
" 929 Richebourg, 1858, grand
" 665 Chambertin, 1858, exceedingly fine
" 666 La Loche, 1858, ditto
" 910 Romanée, 1858, perfect
" 731 Clos-Vougeot, 1858, very fine but not equal to the Romanée.

THOMAS GEORGE SHAW
extract from his cellar notebook, quoted in *Wine, the Vine and the Cellar*, 1863

To compare the magnificent harmony of a fine Bordeaux to a flight of alexandrines is to pay it a doubtful compliment ... for the genius of no great wine is less emphatic, declamatory or monotonous. Grandeur it has, and in high degree, but I find the 'scansion' of Bordeaux, if scansion there must be, ranges from the Horatian to the Miltonic, from the rippling lyrics of Herrick to the sway and surge of Swinburne in the infinite variety of its scope; the 'rhythm' of its incarnadine burden, the lilt of splendid majesty, never the din of rant drowning the creaking of the buskins ...

> MORTON SHAND
> writing in the 1920s 'baroque style'

I was convinced forty years ago – and the conviction remains to this day – that in wine tasting and wine-talk there is an enormous amount of humbug.

> THOMAS GEORGE SHAW
> *Wine, the Vine and the Cellar*, 1863

Deep colour and big shaggy nose. Rather a jumbly, untidy sort of wine, with fruitiness shooting off one way, firmness another and body pushing about underneath. It will be as comfortable and as comforting as the 1961 Nuits St-Georges once it has pulled its ends in and settled down.

> from the wine catalogues of GERALD ASHER

It was golden in colour, suave and yet virile, as if a breeze of the sea had swept the grape and the ghost of its tang still clung and mingled with the bloom.

> WYNDHAM LEWIS
> *On Straw and Other Conceits*

'It is a little, shy wine like a gazelle.'
'Like a leprechaun.'
'Dappled, in a tapestry meadow.'
'Like a flute by still water.'
' …And this is a wise old wine.'
'A prophet in a cave.'
' …And this is a necklace of pearls on a white neck.'
'Like a swan.'
'Like the last unicorn …'
'Ought we to be drunk *every* night?' Sebastian asked one
    morning.
'Yes, I think so.'
'I think so too.'
>   EVELYN WAUGH
>   *Brideshead Revisited*

Lords are lordliest in their wine.
>   JOHN MILTON
>   'Samson Agonistes'

Wine-writing should be camped up: the writer should never
like a wine, he should be in love with it; never find a wine
disappointing but identify it as a mortal enemy …
>   AUBERON WAUGH
>   *Waugh on Wine*

A good general rule is to state that the bouquet is better
than the taste, and vice versa.
>   STEPHEN POTTER
>   *One-upmanship*

When it came to writing about wine, I did what almost everybody does – faked it.
ART BUCHWALD

One never tires of summer sunsets; they are always beautiful and yet they never are quite the same ... That is also the secret of the appeal which Claret has for all wine lovers; it is the most perfectly balanced wine and in ever a new garb; harmony without monotony.
ANDRÉ SIMON
A Wine Primer

A great claret is the queen of all natural wines and ... the highest perfection of all wines that have ever been made. It is delicate and harmonious beyond all others.
H. WARNER ALLEN
British wine writer

How I like claret! ... It fills one's mouth with a gushing freshness, then goes down cool and feverless; then, you do not feel it quarrelling with one's liver. No; 'tis rather a peacemaker, and lies as quiet as it did in the grape. Then it is as fragrant as the Queen Bee, and the more ethereal part mounts into the brain, not assaulting the cerebral compartments, like a bully looking for his trull ... but rather walks like Aladdin about his enchanted palace, so gently that you do not feel his step.
KEATS
in a letter, 1819

I find that nearly all my more knowledgeable wine-drinking friends are claret men at heart. One is always wondering whether the wine in one's glass is at its best, or whether it will be better next year.

> ROBIN DON
> *The Compleat Imbiber*, 1971

The English are so much in the habit of using fortified wine, which will keep almost any time, that they are apt to keep pure Burgundies and Clarets beyond the time when they have arrived at their prime, and after when, as Hippocrates said, as they cannot get better they must get worse. Dives therefore should weed his cellar from time to time, and send his surplus to Lazarus.

> DR ROBERT DRUITT
> *Report on Cheap Wines, Their Use in Diet and Medicine*, 1873

Red bordeaux is like the lawful wife: an excellent beverage that goes with every dish and enables one to enjoy one's food. But now and then a man wants a change ...

> FRANK HARRIS
> *My Life and Loves*

Claret breedeth good humours, and is very good for young men with hot stomachs, but is hurtful for all that are of a cold and moist constitution. To rheumy people, it is of all wines most pernicious.

> DR TOBIAS VENNER

Good sound claret ... an agreeable substitute for tea or coffee at breakfast during warm weather ...

> CHARLES TOVEY
> writing in 1862

The managing director of a large hotel ... told me at a banquet ... in regard to claret, that connoisseurs will differ completely as to the value of a particular wine, or year, when the price gets beyond 25s. a bottle. In other words, up to 25s. a bottle you can be sure of getting value for money, but after 25s. you only get individual preference for money. Whereas with German wines you can get quality as to which all connoisseurs will agree, proportionate to prices far exceeding 25s.

> ARNOLD BENNETT
> *Journals*, April 1929

The magistrate, asked whether he preferred claret or burgundy, answered: 'This is a case, madam, in which it is so pleasant to examine the evidence that I always reserve my judgement for another week.'

> BRILLAT-SAVARIN
> *La Physiologie du goût*

If Claret is the queen of natural wines, Burgundy is the king: their places being taken in the other realm of the artificial by Madeira and Port.

> GEORGE SAINTSBURY
> *Notes on a Cellar-Book*

Burgundy was the winiest wine, the central, essential, and typical wine, the soul and greatest common measure of all the kindly wines of the earth.

CHARLES EDWARD MONTAGUE
Judith

Burgundy tastes of cooked grapes.
BORDELAIS PROVERB

On my way to this town [Beaune] I passed the stretch of the Côte d'Or, which, covered with a mellow autumn haze, with the sunshine shimmering through, looked indeed like a golden slope. One regards with a kind of awe the region in which the famous crûs of Burgundy (Vougeot, Chambertin, Nuits, Beaune) are, I was going to say, manufactured. *Adieu paniers; vendanges sont faites!* The vintage was over; the shrunken russet fibres alone clung to their ugly stick. The horizon on the left on the road had a charm, however; there is something picturesque in the big, comfortable shoulders of the Côte.

HENRY JAMES
A Little Tour in France

The new curé ... set about recruiting and converting. But he realized he would have no influence over the men unless he could be rated a good connoisseur of wine, wine being the only concern at Clochemerle. Intelligence was measured by the finesse of the palate. Whoever, on three gulps swished round the gums, could not say: 'Brouilly, Fleurie, Morgon or Juliénas', was considered a prize idiot by these fervent vine growers ...

Inspired with evangelical conviction, he began to frequent the inn and to take a glass of wine with one and the other of Torbayon's customers ...

The system did not bring a single soul back to God. But Ponosse acquired real proficiency in the matter of wines, and thereby gained the respect of the vine growers of Clochemerle ... In fifteen years, Ponosse's nose flowered magnificently, becoming a huge beaujolais nose, the shade of which was somewhere between canons' purple and cardinalate crimson. His nose inspired confidence in the region.

> GABRIEL CHEVALLIER
> *Clochemerle*

The 11 of November is St Martins day, a very merry day in France. They passe it in eating, drinking and singing excessivelie. Every one tastes his new wine that day, and in tasting it takes too much.

> SIR JOHN LAUDER
> *Journals*, 1665-76

At Pommard and Voulenay, I observed them eating good wheat bread; at Meursault, rye. I asked the reason of this difference. They told me that the white wines fail in quality much oftener than the red and remain on hand. The farmer, therefore, cannot afford to feed his laborers so well. At Meursault, only white wines are made, because there is too much stone for the red. On such slight circumstances depends the condition of man!

    THOMAS JEFFERSON
    Travel Journals

I have never managed to like white Burgundy, though some of its humbler cousins from the Loire, especially Sancerre, please me greatly; the limitless world of German wine would take several score lifetimes to explore properly, but I have been doing what I can in thirty-odd years of my present span; though I will often seek an excuse to order red Burgundy (O that Richebourg, and my youth, long ago!), in the end I will always turn to claret, the noblest family in the great people of wine.

    BERNARD LEVIN
    Enthusiasms

The point about white Burgundies is that ... they so closely resemble a blend of cold chalk soup and alum cordial with an additive or two to bring it to the colour of children's pee.

    KINGSLEY AMIS
    The Green Man

Even those who have forty years' old Port in their cellars had much better drink it. But my Hermitage [of 1846, drunk in 1886] showed not the slightest mark or presage of enfeeblement. It was ... not a delicate wine ... But it was the *manliest* French wine I ever drank; and age had softened and polished all that might have been rough in the manliness of its youth ...

GEORGE SAINTSBURY
Notes on a Cellar-Book

Moselle is like the girl of fourteen to eighteen: light, quick on the tongue, with an exquisite, evanescent perfume, but little body. It may be used constantly and in quantities, but must be taken young.

FRANK HARRIS
My Life and Loves

'Great thing about Moselle,' he continued ..., 'it's the perfect wine to serve before a claret. A lot of people serve a Rhine wine instead, but that's because they don't know any better. A Rhine wine will kill a delicate claret, you know that? It's barbaric to serve a Rhine before a claret. But a Moselle – ah! – a Moselle is exactly right.'

ROALD DAHL
Taste

In many places of Germany there growes wery good wines, in some none at all. The Rhenish wine which growes on the renouned Rhein, on which standes so many brave townes, is weill enough knowen. They sometymes sell their wine by the weight as the livre or pound ... This they ar necessitate to do in the winter, when it freizes so that they most break it wt great mattocks and axes.

> SIR JOHN LAUDER
> *Journals*, 1665-76

Rhineland is wineland.
> GERMAN PROVERB

Rhine wine, fine wine.
> GERMAN PROVERB

The best wines grow just about the château, but though this estate [Hochheim] gives its name to all the white wine of the neighbourhood, very little, if any, of the real Hock reaches England. Indeed I am told it is a wine used almost as a medicine. The Johannisberg wine is the real 'nectar of the Rhine', as the Germans term it ... The hill on which it is raised is sheltered by the bend of the Rhine and by the range of the Taunus Mountains from all the harsh winds, and the sun shines on it all day long. This lovely region of the Rheingau is spoken of with ecstasy by the Germans and one of their writers calls it 'a piece of heaven that has fallen upon the earth'.

> WASHINGTON IRVING
> *Journals*, 1820

When I was ordering a bottle of hock we laughed because the waiter told us that the price had been reduced since 1914, as it was now an unpopular wine. The hock had its happy effect, and soon we were agreeing that the Front Line was the only place where one could get away from the War.

SIEGFRIED SASSOON
Memoirs of an Infantry Officer

Bright with bold wine
From the old Rhine,
Take this goblet in thy hand!
Quaff the Rhenish bumper gleely.
Let thy true blood flow as freely,
For our German fatherland.
BURSCHEN MELODY.

The Germans are exceedingly fond of Rhine wines; they are put up in tall, slender bottles, and are considered a pleasant beverage. One tells them from vinegar by the label.

MARK TWAIN
A Tramp Abroad

In Spain, that land of Monks and Apes,
The thing called Wine doth come from grapes,
But on the noble River Rhine,
The thing called Gripes doth come from Wine!
COLERIDGE
'Rheinwein'

If you wanted to open a sausage shop – hang giant liverwursts and salamis right in the window – a terrific name for the shop would be Gewürztraminer … Which wine snob, I ask you, will order a Schloss Vollrads – a sound likened to a tyre going flat – when he could have an Amarone and a thousand violins?

LEONARD BERNSTEIN
The Official Guide to Wine Snobbery

Oh some are fond of Spanish wine, and some are fond of French …

JOHN MASEFIELD
'Captain Stratton's Fancy'

When Sir Robert Walpole advised the King to take Lady Deloraine [as his mistress] till Madam Walmoden could be brought over His Majesty said she stank of Spanish wine so abominably of late that he could not bear her.

LORD HERVEY
Memoirs of the Reign of George II

The Spanish wine, my God, it is foul, catpiss is champagne compared, this is the sulphurous urination of some aged horse.

D.H.LAWRENCE
- in a letter, 1929

Bad Spanish wine furs the tongue, turns the breath sour, upsets the stomach and produces a murderous hangover.

AUBERON WAUGH
Waugh on Wine

Early next morning, when I came out at the hotel door to pursue my journey, I found my friend waiting with one of those immense bottles in which the Italian peasants store their wine – a bottle holding some half-dozen gallons – bound round with basket-work for greater safety on the journey.

CHARLES DICKENS
The Uncommercial Traveller

The wines were strange, dark and repulsive with various chemical additives, what the Italians call *vini lavorati*, worked on, primitive harbingers of the more sophisticated, doctored wines which rarely contain any grapes at all … but like meths drinkers we enjoyed them better than no alcohol at all.

ERIC NEWBY
Love and War in the Apennines

There was one more formative experience, and that was Italy. For a time it was Apulia, the heel of Italy, where even in peacetime the wines are indifferent, and southern Italy at the time was cruelly deprived and devastated by war, even beyond its usual state of grinding poverty. But it was still a country where wine was a part of life – we picked the grapes from roadside vineyards to quench our thirst as the Eighth Army clanked and rumbled its way northwards in a cloud of dust – and where men grew wine as a matter of course, and put grimy carafes of it on the table at every meal, equally as a matter of course.

CYRIL RAY
Ray on Wine

Some of us, kind old Pagans, watch with dread the shadows falling on the age: how the unconquerable worm invades the sunny terraces of France, and Bordeaux is no more, and the Rhône a mere Arabia Petraea. Château Neuf is dead, and I have never tasted it; Hermitage – a hermitage indeed from all life's sorrows – lies expiring by the river ... It is not Pan only; Bacchus, too, is dead.

... The new lands, already weary of producing gold, begin to green with vineyards. A nice point in human history falls to be decided by Californian and Australian wines.

ROBERT LOUIS STEVENSON
written at the height of phylloxera in the early 1880s

For the richest and best
Is the wine of the West,
That grows by the Beautiful River;
Whose sweet perfume
Fills all the room
With a benison on the giver ...

There grows no vine
By the haunted Rhine,
By Danube or Guadalquivir,
Nor an island or cape,
That bears such a grape
As grows by the Beautiful River.

H.W.LONGFELLOW
'Catawba Wine'

A Bordeaux wine merchant called on me the other day, and, in order to improve the occasion, I had up a bottle of Auldana, and asked him what it was. He said that I must pardon him for his want of familiarity with Burgundy, but he supposed it to be Pommard, and greatly he stared when I told him it was Australian, for no Frenchman can conceive of any wine that is not French.

> DR ROBERT DRUITT
> *Report on Cheap Wines, Their Use in Diet and Medicine*, 1873

All drinks stand cap in hand,
In presence of old Sherry.
Then let us drink old Sack, old Sack, boys,
Which makes us blithe and merry.

> PASQUIL
> 17th century

If I had a thousand sons, the first human principle I would teach them should be, to forswear thin potations and to addict themselves to sack.

> SHAKESPEARE
> Falstaff in *Henry IV*, Part 2

And the permission to drink a glass or two of pure sherry being accorded to Pen by Doctor Goodenough, the Major told with almost tears in his eyes how his noble friend the Marquis of Steyne ... had ordered any quantity of his precious, his priceless Amontillado, that had been a present from King Ferdinand to the noble Marquis, to be placed at the disposal of Mr Arthur Pendennis. The widow and Laura tasted it with respect (though they didn't in the least like the bitter flavour), but the invalid was greatly invigorated by it.

    THACKERAY
    Pendennis

Pale Sherry at a funeral, golden at a wedding, brown at any time ... One man's Sherry is another man's poison ... Let your humour and your Sherry both be 'dry'.

    advice from *Punch*, quoted by
    CHARLES TOVEY
    Wit, Wisdom and Morals Distilled from Bacchus, 1878

I once even attempted a fully graded menu and wine-list with sherry only to fill the latter – a 'sherry dinner' ... Manzanilla with oysters; Montilla with soup and fish; an Amontillado with entrées and roast; an Amoroso or some such wine with sweets; and for after dinner, the oldest and brownest of 'old browns', say Brown Bristol Milk.

    GEORGE SAINTSBURY
    Notes on a Cellar-Book

Sherry is a self-willed wine which gives a good deal of trouble to its guardians during its early years: it must have its own way, but, like many a difficult child, when Sherry reaches the age of sweet reasonableness, it is the most amenable of all wines, the only one that will not let its nose be put out by being left overnight and even for some days in a decanter; the only one to put up cheerfully with cigarette smoke and over-scented women.

    ANDRÉ SIMON
    A Wine Primer

In England, sherry is the symbol of hospitality at home ...
An invitation to 'come over for a glass of sherry' promises a
relaxed communion of friends, comfortable shoes, an old
sweater, an occasion that no one will be using as part of
life's strategic game plan.

> GERALD ASHER
> *On Wine*

He sits in a beautiful parlour,
With hundreds of books on the wall,
He drinks a great deal of Marsala,
But never gets tipsy at all.

> EDWARD LEAR
> 'How Pleasant to Know Mr Lear'

Greatest of all Madeiras, Malmsey, in which great
bottle-age transforms a quintessence of sweetness into a
profound magnificence of ambrosial immortality such as the
gods in the Golden Age drank in Olympus after they had
quenched their thirst with nectar, is perhaps the finest wine
in the world.

> H. WARNER ALLEN
> British wine writer

The unearned increment of my grandfather's Madeira ...

> JAMES RUSSELL LOWELL
> on his sufferings with the gout

Should auld acquaintance be forgot
And never thought upon
Let's hae a waught o'Malaga
For auld lang syne.
For auld lang syne my dear
For auld lang syne,
Let's hae a waught o'Malaga
For auld lang syne.

Alternative version of Auld Lang Syne collected
in 1788 by
ROBERT BURNS

Be sometimes to your country true
Have once the public good in view;
Bravely despise champagne at court
and choose to dine at home on port.

Patriotic injunction in support of the Methuen
treaty with Portugal in 1703

Sir Hercules Langreish, on being asked, 'Have you finished
all that Port (three bottles) without assistance' answered,
'No – not quite that; I had the assistance of a bottle of
Madeira.'

CHARLES TOVEY
Wit, Wisdom, and Morals, Distilled from Bacchus

All wine would be Port if it could.
PORTUGUESE PROVERB

For Port ... is incomparable when good. It is not a wine-of-all-work like Sherry .... It has not the almost feminine grace and charm of Claret; the transcendental qualities of Burgundy and Madeira; the immediate inspiration of Champagne ... But it strengthens while it gladdens as no other wine can do; and there is something about it which must have been created in pre-established harmony with the best English character.

> GEORGE SAINTSBURY
> *Notes on a Cellar-Book*

It must appear strange to those who have always considered Port as the only wine suited for 'John Bull' and his climate, to learn how it was forced into use, only a century and a half ago ... Although exceedingly fine when originally of a good vintage and of sufficient age, it may justly be objected that owing to the large portion of Brandy added even to the best ... the wine is rendered so powerful, that none but Englishmen can drink it.

> THOMAS GEORGE SHAW
> In a letter to *The Times* in 1851

Claret is the liquor for boys, port for men ...

> SAMUEL JOHNSON
> Boswell's *Life of Johnson*

Port ... the milk of donhood.

> MAX BEERBOHM

Jones : ' I say, Brown, things are deuced bad in the City.'
Brown : ' Then I'm deuced glad I'm at Epsom.'

(From a drawing by John Leech in ' Punch.')

3 August 1790 I drank but very little Wine Yesterday or today only 2. or 3. Glasses. I used myself before and all last Winter to near a Pint of Port Wine every Day and I now believe did me much harm …

26 December 1794 I drank plentifully of Port Wine after dinner, instead of one Glass, drank 7. or 8. Wine Glasses, and it seemed to do me much good, being better for it …

29 March 1797 Mr Thorne came to see Nancy this Morning. He strongly recommends Port Wine and to drink rather more than less. She drank to day between a Pint and a Quart without having the lest effect upon the Brain. She has not drank less than a Pint for many Days …

    JAMES WOODFORDE
    The Diary of a Country Parson

An old gourmet who's grown somewhat stout,
Felt a twinge and much feared it was gout.
'If I drink now,' he thought,
'Three whole bottles of port,
It surely will settle the doubt.'
    YORICK

19 May 1870 All the afternoon I had a bad face ache and could enjoy nothing. I tried laudanum and port wine, but nothing did any good ...

1 March 1871 After dinner last night Mr V. kindly anxious to cure my face ache made me drink four large glasses of port. The consequence was that all night and all today I have been groaning with a bursting raging splitting sick headache.

> REV. FRANCIS KILVERT
> *Diary*

The Gentleman did take a drop too much,
(Though there are many such)
And took more Port than was exactly portable.
> THOMAS HOOD
> 'The Green Man'

Garlic port
Chop a pound of garlic, put it into a litre measure of old Port, and let it macerate for twenty days. Begin with half a liqueur glass every evening before the soup course, then slowly increase the dose to one or two liqueur glasses.

This beverage is a sovereign remedy for chronic bronchitis.
> TOULOUSE-LAUTREC
> *L'Art de la cuisine*

He was a great gourmand. He always had on him a small grater and a nutmeg with which he scented the ports he drank ... He tasted old vintages as a connoisseur.
> PAUL LECLERCQ
> French poet, writing about Toulouse-Lautrec

I question if keeping it does it much good
After ten years in bottle, and three in the wood.
R.H. BARHAM
Ingoldsby Legends

The gem of the three was a '73, which had been allowed to remain in wood till it was eight or nine years old, and in bottle for about as much longer before I bought it. It had lost very little colour and not much body of the best kind; but if there ever was any devil in its soul that soul had thoroughly exorcised the intruder and replaced him with an angel. I had my headquarters in Reading at the time, and a member of my family was being attended by the late Mr Oliver Maurice ... He once appeared rather doubtful when I told him that I had given his patient port; so I made him taste this. He drank it as a port should be drunk – a trial of the bouquet; a slow sip; a rather larger and slightly less slow one, and so on; but never a gulp; and during the drinking his face exchanged its usual bluff and almost brusque aspect for the peculiar blandness ... which good wine gives to worthy countenances. And when he set the glass down he said ... '*That* won't do her any harm.' But I am not entirely certain that in his heart of hearts he did not think it rather wasted on a lady.
GEORGE SAINTSBURY
Notes on a Cellar-Book

There was a young lady at court
Who said to the King, with a snort:
'Was it humour or shyness
That prompted your Highness
To put Spanish Fly in my port?'
    C.D. CUDMORE

Women still regard port as their natural enemy.
    AUBERON WAUGH
    Waugh on Wine

A pint of old Port and a devilled biscuit can hurt no man.
    R.S. SURTEES
    Handley Cross

Senatorial Port! we say. We cannot say that of any other wine. Port is deep-sea deep. It is in its flavour deep; mark the difference. It is like a classic tragedy, organic in conception ... Neither of Hermitage nor of Hock can you say that it is the blood of those long years, retaining the strength of youth with the wisdom of age ... Port speaks in sentences of wisdom, Burgundy sings the inspired Ode.
    GEORGE MEREDITH
    The Egoist

'Do you drink port or claret, Mr Sponge?' asked Jawleyford, preparing to push whichever he preferred over to him.

'I'll take a little port, *first*, if you please,' replied our friend – as much as to say, 'I'll finish off with claret.'

'You'll find that very good, I expect,' said Mr Jawleyford, passing the bottle to him; 'it's '20 wine – very rare wine to get now – was a very rich fruity wine, and was a long time before it came into drinking. Connoisseurs would give any money for it.'

'It has still a good deal of body,' observed Sponge, turning off a glass and smacking his lips, at the same time holding the glass up to the candle to see the oily mark it made on the side.

'Good sound wine – good sound wine,' said Mr Jawleyford, 'Have plenty lighter, if you like.' The light wine was made by watering the strong.

'Oh, no, thank you,' replied Mr Sponge, 'Oh, no, thank you. I like good strong military port.'

'So do I,' said Mr Jawleyford, 'so do I; only unfortunately it doesn't like me – am obliged to drink claret. When I was in the Bumperkin yeomanry we drank nothing but port.'

R.S. SURTEES
Mr Sponge's Sporting Tour

When rectors drank Port Wine,
When no man talked of grace,
What jolly days were those!
Ah! then a parson's face
Displayed a parson's nose, –
A parson's nose of red,
Which gloriously did shine,
Supremely strong of head,
When rectors drank Port Wine...
    verses from *Punch*, 1870s

The gentle fair on nervous tea relied,
Champagne the courtier drinks, the spleen to chase,
The colonel Burgundy, and Port his Grace ...
    GEORGE CRABBE
    Inebriety

101

Burgundy for kings, champagne for duchesses, and claret for gentlemen.
FRENCH PROVERB

'There are ... certain geographical boundaries in the land of literature, and you may judge tolerably well of an author's popularity by the wine his bookseller gives him. An author crosses the port line about the 3rd edition, and gets into claret; and when he has reached the 6th or 7th, he may revel in champagne and burgundy.'
WASHINGTON IRVING
on a literary dinner in London in *Tales of a Traveller*

When fortune frowns, and friends forsake,
And faith in love is dead –
When man has nothing left to stake,
To hope, nor yet to dread –
One godlike pleasure doth remain,
Worth all the joys he's lost –
The glorious vintage of Champagne,
From silver goblets tossed!
CHARLES TOVEY
Wit, Wisdom, and Morals, Distilled from Bacchus

Here's to champagne, the drink divine
That makes us forget our troubles;
It's made of a dollar's worth of wine
And three dollars' worth of bubbles
ANON

I could not conjure up one melancholy fancy upon a mutton chop and a glass of champagne.

> JEROME K. JEROME
> *Idle Thoughts of an Idle Fellow*

A single glass of champagne imparts a feeling of exhilaration ... A bottle produces the contrary effect.

> WINSTON CHURCHILL

I am a beer teetotaller, not a champagne teetotaller.

> GEORGE BERNARD SHAW

No government could survive without champagne. Champagne in the throats of our diplomatic people is like oil in the wheels of an engine.

> JOSEPH DARGENT
> French vintner, in 1955

Gentlemen, in the little moment that remains to us between the crisis and the catastrophe, we may as well drink a glass of champagne.

> PAUL CLAUDEL
> in a speech in 1931

Mistress-like, its brilliance vain,
Highly capricious and inane ...

> PUSHKIN
> who drank champagne with everything

The most agreeable and (to me) most pernicious of all alcoholic liquids, champagne ...

> ARNOLD BENNETT
> *Journals*, April 1929

A man who sets you down to a driblet of champagne – who gives you a couple of beggarly glasses between the courses, and winks to John who froths up the liquor in your glass, and screws up the remainder of the bottle for his master's next day's drinking – such a man is an impostor and despicable snob ... If money is an object to you, drink water ... but if there is to be champagne, have no stint of it, in the name of Bacchus ... When people have had plenty of champagne, they fancy they have been treated liberally. If you wish to save, save upon your hocks, sauternes, and moselles, which count for nothing, but disappear down careless throats like so much toast and water ...

Incomparably the best champagne I know is to be found in England. It is the most doctored, the most brandied, the most barley-sugared, the most *winy* wine in the world.

> THACKERAY
> *Miscellaneous Papers*

The sound of thy explosive cork, Champagne, has, by some strange witchery, of a sudden taught men the sweet music of speech. A murmur as of a rising storm runs round the table: badinage commences, flirtations flourish ... We might tell of breakfasts, and of suppers, suddenly converted from Saharas of intolerable dullness into oases of smiles and laughter by the appearance of Champagne.

> CHARLES TOVEY
> *Wit, Wisdom, and Morals, Distilled from Bacchus*

For two intimates, lovers or comrades, to spend a quiet evening with a magnum, drinking no aperitif before, nothing but a glass of cognac after – that is the ideal … The worst time is that dictated by convention, in a crowd, in the early afternoon, at a wedding reception.

> EVELYN WAUGH
> New York *Vogue*, 1937

'Barley water!' Bingo's voice was vibrant with scorn. 'What on earth's the good of barley water? How can you expect to be the masterful wooer on stuff like that? I should be a bachelor today if I hadn't had the prudence to fill myself to the brim with about a quart of mixed champagne and stout before asking Rosie to come registrar's-officing with me. That's what you want, champagne and stout. It'll make a new man of you.'

> P.G. WODEHOUSE
> *Tales from the Drones Club*

'Champagne isn't worth a copper unless it's iced – is it Colonel?

'Vy, I don't know – I carn't say I like it so werry cold; it makes my teeth chatter, and cools my courage as it gets below – champagne certainly gives one werry gentlemanly ideas, but for a continuance, I don't know but I should prefer mild hale.'

> R.S. SURTEES
> *Mr Jorrocks's Jaunts and Jollities*

'You know my way with the women; champagne's the thing; make 'em drink, make 'em talk; – make 'em talk, make 'em do anything.'

> THACKERAY
> *The Paris Sketch Book*

Champagne: the great civilizer …

> TALLEYRAND

Start her on champagne, boy,
but break her into hock –
That's the only rule of life
that's steady as a rock.

> A.P. HERBERT

Algernon: Why is it that at a bachelor's establishment the servants invariably drink the champagne? I ask merely for information.

Lane: I attribute it to the superior quality of the wine, sir. I have often observed that in married households the champagne is rarely of a first-rate brand.

> OSCAR WILDE
> The Importance of Being Earnest

Champagne has the taste of an apple peeled with a steel knife.

> ALDOUS HUXLEY
> *Time Must Have a Stop*

When the cloth was removed, the butler brought in a huge silver vessel of rare and curious workmanship, which he placed before the Squire. Its appearance was hailed with acclamation; being the Wassail Bowl, so renowned in Christmas festivity. The contents had been prepared by the Squire himself; for it was a beverage in the skilful mixture of which he particularly prided himself; alleging that it was too abstruse and complex for the comprehension of an ordinary servant. It was a potation, indeed, that might well make the heart of a toper leap within him; being composed of the richest and raciest wines, highly spiced and sweetened, with roasted apples bobbing about the surface.

The old gentleman's whole countenance beamed with a serene look of indwelling delight, as he stirred this mighty bowl. Having raised it to his lips, with a hearty wish of a merry Christmas to all present, he sent it brimming round the board, for every one to follow his example ...

I found the tide of wine and wassail fast gaining on the dry land of sober judgment. The company grew merrier and louder as their jokes grew duller.

WASHINGTON IRVING
Old Christmas